CATEGORY PIRATES

How To Build Your First (Crazy Profitable) Business As A Teenager

18 Radical Ideas For 18-Year-Old Entrepreneurs And Younger

First edition

ISBN: 978-1-956934-24-3

Narration by Nicolas Cole
Narration by Eddie Yoon
Narration by Christopher Lochhead

This book was professionally typeset on Reedsy.
Find out more at reedsy.com

Contents

Meet The Pirates

What is Category Pirates?

Category Pirates is the authority on Category Creation and Category Design.

Every Wednesday (ish), we publish a "mini-book" for the radically different—who want to see, design, and dominate categories of consequence.

Topics include:

- How to create new categories and redesign old ones.
- The Magic Triangle, The 9 Levers, The Category Design Scorecard, and dozens of frameworks for how to create and design new categories in the world.
- Case studies for how successful companies have successful created and/or redesigned existing categories (and where other companies have gone wrong).
- Motivational examples of the power of creating and investing in category creators such as Tesla, Netflix, Amazon, Airbnb, and more.

Every new edition of the newsletter goes directly to your inbox.

- Free subscribers receive one out of every four "mini-books."
- Paying subscribers receive "mini-books" every week.

"Why join the Navy if you can be a pirate?" - Steve Jobs

If you are reading this "mini-book," that means you stumbled upon Category Pirates somewhere else (like Amazon). Instead of buying & reading each "mini-book" on its own, we encourage you to subscribe and receive each "mini-book" in your inbox each week (you also receive access to our entire archive of previously published "mini-books").

You can subscribe to Category Pirates here: https://categorypirates.substack.com

Meet The Pirates: Eddie Yoon

Eddie Yoon has written more on category strategy for Harvard Business Review than any other person.

Eddie is the founder of EddieWouldGrow, LLC, a think tank and advisory firm on growth strategy, and Co-Creator of Category Pirates.

Previously, he was one of the senior partners at The Cambridge Group, a strategy consulting firm. His work over the past two decades has driven over **$8 billion dollars of annual incremental revenue.** In particular, 8 of his clients have doubled or tripled in revenue in less than 8 years. Eddie is one of the world's leading experts on finding and monetizing Superconsumers to grow and create new categories.

He is the author of the book ***Superconsumers: A Simple,***

Speedy and Sustainable Path to Superior Growth (Harvard Business School Press, 2016). His book was named as one of the Best Business Books of 2017 by Strategy & Business. Eddie is also the author of over 100 articles, including "Make Your Best Customers Even Better" (Harvard Business Review magazine, March 2014) and "Why It Pays to Be a Category Creator" (Harvard Business Review magazine, March 2013). Additionally, he has appeared on CNBC and MSNBC, and been quoted in *The Wall Street Journal*, *The Economist*, and *Forbes* for his predictions on future category potential of publicly traded companies, as well as been a keynote speaker at industry-leading events in the U.S., Canada, Kenya, Australia, New Zealand, Denmark, the UK and Japan.

Eddie holds an AB in Political Science and Economics from the University of Chicago. Born and raised in Hawaii, he went to the Punahou School in Honolulu. Today, Eddie lives in Chicago with his wife and three children.

Meet The Pirates: Nicolas Cole

Nicolas Cole is one of the most prolific digital writers in the world.

"Cole" as he's known, is an author, viral writer, ghostwriter, and serial "writing entrepreneur." He is the Co-Founder of Ship 30 for 30 (a cohort-based community to help people start writing online), Digital Press (a ghostwriting agency for founders, executives, and industry leaders), and Category Pirates. He's been writing online since he was 17 years old—and to date has accumulated hundreds of millions of views on his work.

In 2015, Cole became the #1 most-read writer on Quora (a Question/Answer website with more than 300 million users). And in 2016, he was one of *Inc Magazine's* Top 10 contributing writers, bringing in millions of page views for the publication. His work has been republished all across the Internet, including: *TIME, Forbes, Fortune, Business Insider, CNBC, Harvard Business Review*, and more.

Over the years, Cole has written more than 3,000 articles online, as well as thousands more under other people's names. He has ghostwritten for hundreds of Silicon Valley founders, Fortune 500 executives, renowned venture capitalists and angel investors, Grammy-winning musicians, Olympic athletes, *New York Times* best-selling authors, and more.

Finally, Cole is the author of the best-selling book, *The Art & Business of Online Writing*, which has become a must-read in the digital publishing world.

He lives in Los Angeles but will forever be from Chicago.

Meet The Pirates: Christopher Lochhead

Christopher Lochhead is a multi-time #1 best-selling Amazon author, #1 Apple podcaster, Top 1% business newsletter creator, and is best known as a "godfather" of Category Design.

He is on a mission to help people design a different future. And ALL of his work is co-created with legendary friends and partners—who he is beyond grateful for.

Christopher's two books, *Play Bigger* and *Niche Down*, were the first texts written on the management discipline of Category Design. And the Category Pirates newsletter is the #1 paid newsletter on the subject, with the Category Pirates "mini-books" consecutively charting at #1 on Amazon. Christopher is also the host of Follow Your Different, a #1 charting business dialogue podcast, and Lochhead on Marketing, a #1 charting Marketing and Category Design podcast.

Christopher is a dyslexic paperboy from Montreal who got thrown out of school at 18 years old. With few other options, he became an entrepreneur, then three-time Silicon Valley public company CMO (Mercury Interactive, Scient, Vantive), and an investor & advisor to over 50 venture-backed startups.

The Marketing Journal calls him "one of the best minds in marketing," NBA legend Bill Walton calls him a "quasar," The Economist calls him "off-putting to some," and some podcast reviewers think he is "overrated" and "not worth it." Podcaster Neil Pearlberg calls Follow Your Different "the worst business podcast," and Podcast Magazine calls Follow Your Different "the best business podcast."

Christopher believes if you're lucky enough to make it to the top of a mountain, you should throw down a rope. So that's what he's trying to do.

You can subscribe to Category Pirates here: https://categorypirates.substack.com

What Other Pirates Have To Say

"If you want to know how to change the world, read Category Pirates. You don't win championships by just being normal."
—Bill Walton, NBA Hall of Fame Legend

"Every Category Pirates edition is of immense value. Seriously, it's like a $100,000 MBA with every read."
—Steve Olsher, Founder of Podcast Magazine

"When Category Pirates pops up in my inbox, I don't click it right away. I schedule deliberate time, make coffee, and sit in a comfortable chair to read the entire thing. Simply put, this is the most compelling business/marketing letter out."
—Drew Reggie, Founder of Fly Me To The Fun

"The value Category Pirates provides is amazing! I am blown away by the quality of their content and how much I learn each week. Reading their newsletter is better than any marketing class in college."
—Mike Flynn, Founder of Engenius Learning

"Category Pirates has fundamentally changed how I perceive business. It's unique frameworks have shifted my approach, helped me Name & Claim an emerging category of my own ('cofounder therapy'), and even refined my investment strategy as well (investing through a category lens). All in all, Category Pirates has accelerated my

understanding of business 10x."
—Dr. Matthew Jones, Founder of Cofounder Clarity

"Category Pirates is a fantastic source of new ideas, thinking and data on Category Creation for me. But it's also one of the best ways to align my executive team. I regularly forward letters to my team, to make sure we are charting the right path to creating this amazing Beauty Health category."
—Clint Carnell, CEO of the Beauty Health Company

"I love these outstanding mini-books from Category Pirates. I can't wait every week to read them. I have used the Point of View and examples on category creation with so many people in Colgate!"
—Mukul Deoras, President of Asia and prior CMO of Colgate-Palmolive

Introduction

Dear Teenage Pirates,

Don't listen to most people (especially your Native Analog parents).

Minimum wage jobs suck.

Most parents, at some point or another, all say the same thing: "You have to get a *real* job."

A *real* job, it turns out, is just something that involves manual labor for low pay—which is likely what they had to go through when they were your age. (*"When I was your age...I had to deliver 10,000 newspapers, in the morning, through the snow, with no boots!"*) This is exactly what Pirate Cole's parents said to him when he was a teenager, getting paid $25 per hour to write World of Warcraft walkthrough guides for a gaming website. When he told his parents how he was starting to make money (thinking they'd be proud), instead they said, "No, you have to get a *real* job, Cole. Something that will teach you work ethic, and how to put in a little *elbow grease.*" They made him take a job as an ice cream scooper at the local Coldstone Creamery—which paid him 50% less than what he was making writing articles about his favorite video game online, and required him to wear an apron, scrub melted ice cream trays, and mop the back office and bathroom floors.

Were his parents right? Did working an *elbow grease* Native Analog job teach him anything valuable?

Not really. It just confirmed what he already knew (scooping ice cream for minimum wage sucks), and postponed what he ultimately wanted to do (which is write online).

Today, Pirate Cole is one of the most-read and highest paid digital writers on the planet.

Part of being an entrepreneur of any kind means going against the grain. (Pirate Christopher started his first businesses while a teenager, back when most people thought entrepreneur was a French word for "unemployed.") But being a teenage entrepreneur today means acknowledging (and having compassion for the fact) that your Native Analog parents are probably not going to understand your Native Digital pursuits. Your dad has no idea what an NFT is. Your mom can barely assemble a Spotify playlist, let alone make sense of why you think creating video thumbnails in photoshop for YouTubers is a replacement for college and can be turned into a highly profitable digital business. (Huge category here, by the way.) And how could they understand? They didn't grow up in a time where you could start a 95% margin digital goods business with nothing except an Internet connection and a laptop or smartphone.

So, Step 1: when your parents say, "That will never work" or "You need to get a *real* job," it's important that you look them in the eye, tell them you love them, and then go right on building what you know makes complete sense in your Native Digital world.

Prove them wrong, in the best way.

Now, that said, we don't want any angry letters from parents shouting, "YOU TOLD OUR KID TO JUST DO WHATEVER THE HELL SHE WANTS." If you love playing Fortnite or are absolutely obsessed with TikTok, don't just be a consumer. Turn your passion into a crazy profitable business—and don't worry, we're going to explain to you exactly how.

Step 2:

Start Native Digital. Don't even think about doing anything in the Analog world.

The only thing that sucks as much as a minimum wage job these days is most Analog jobs.

Obviously, the world still needs plumbers. And construction workers. And warehouse managers. And piano teachers. And burger flippers. And highway patrollers. And bank tellers. And cashiers.

But more and more of these jobs are either being automated and digitized away, or becoming Native Analog-Digital hybrids (these jobs are what Elon Musk is designing the Tesla bot to do). Why only teach piano lessons to the students in your town when you can teach students from all over the country remotely? Why only draw up construction plans for new projects in your city when you can draw up construction plans for buildings anywhere in the world? That's point A.

Point B is: Analog businesses are hard. They require you to put on pants. They involve lifting stuff, moving stuff, managing physical "stuff." But most importantly, they are far less profitable. The average profit margin for a small business in North America is around 7%. Restaurants are even lower, with an average profit margin of 3-6%. Meanwhile, digital businesses can be started (and scaled to six, seven, even eight figures in revenue) with almost no overhead: no rent, no employees, and no fixed costs (like needing to buy lawn mowers for your landscaping business, or t-shirts for your clothing business). Aside from a computer and/or smartphone, few low-cost SaaS tools like a website builder and email marketing platform, and fees from a credit card processing tool like Stripe, your business can operate at an 80% or even 90%+ profit margin.

Which means you can easily be profitable Day 1.

Besides, as a Native Digital, the vast majority of your skills are probably "digital" anyway, which means you're better off trying to monetize what you know and know well—opposed to teaching yourself how to use a socket wrench.

If you can build a (crazy profitable) digital business for yourself as a teenager, you'll be set for life.

Pirate Eddie ran the numbers...

- If you invest $30,000 in the Vanguard S&P 500 Index Fund by age 18, assuming modest 7% returns then *you'll have a little over $700,000 by the time you retire at age 65.*
- If you invest $30,000 in more forward-leaning companies and produce returns closer to a Venture Capitalist (15+%), *you'll have $32 million dollars by the time you retire.*
- And if you invest in Category Queens like say Microsoft or Apple who go on to capture the lion's share of category economics and average an annual return of 25%, *you'll have $2 billion dollars by the time you retire.* (We know that's not enough to live on, but it's certainly a start.)

This is one of the greatest areas of high school education malpractice. (Translation: they should teach this in school!) Social Security and other government safety nets will not be available for Native Digitals like you. The government is not coming to the rescue. You're on your own. The good news is: if you make money and invest aggressively when you're young and let the time value of money do its job, retirement shouldn't be a problem.

Unfortunately, the very notion of focusing on your education and delaying the opportunity to make money now so you can make more money later (and losing a teenager's *time value of money* advantage) is the very reason why there is a retirement crisis today. **It is one of the greatest lies society tells young people.** But if you *work hard now* as a teenager, you will be set in your golden years—allowing you to actually pursue your passion during the bulk of your adult life.

Now, $30,000 might sound like a lot of money, especially as a 14, 15, or 16 year old, but if you break it down, it's not. That's 10 clients each paying you $3,000 per *year* (or a measly $250 per month). Or that's 100 people buying a $300 product. Or 300 people buying a $100 product. And that's if you want to try to make $30,000 in a single year. Can you find 75 people to buy a $100 product per year for 4 years? That's like six people per month.

We think you can.

More importantly, if you can figure out how to produce this very actionable sort of financial outcome for yourself as a teenager, not only will you guarantee yourself a comfortable retirement (which opens up a massive amount of personal freedom for you to enjoy all throughout your life), but you'll also build a skill most people never learn—which is how to engineer financial outcomes and build businesses out of thin air.

And once you learn how to do that, you're set for life.

(Because you can always build another business.)

You can either work to make someone else's dream come true, or you can work to make *your* dream come true.

One last thing: Thinking about thinking is the most important kind of thinking.

What you're not going to find in this mini-book is a Betty Crocker recipe for "3 easy steps to make your first $30,000."

That's not how business works (and anyone who says so is teasing you with a carrot long enough to steal that $20 out of your pocket).

Instead, we are going to give you some laws to live by, guardrails for your thinking, and 18 radical ideas to get you started. If one (or several) of these ideas *sticks* then by all means, run with it. But if none resonate with you, don't sit there and go, "You didn't give me an easy answer" and then give up. Use these ideas as a starting point. They are examples. Let your mind wander a bit. See *what else* they make you think about—and go give it a try.

Ready Player One?

If you are a teenager working an Analog minimum wage job you hate (or can sense, any day now, your parents are going to start nudging you in that direction), this is the path to quitting and paying yourself instead.

ARRRRRRRR!!!!!!!

Radical Idea #1: Be a local business's best (digital) salesperson.

Your biggest opportunity as a teenager today isn't to disregard your fellow Native Analogs, call them "boomers," and leave them behind.

Remember: those Boomers have an estimated $2.6 trillion (with a capital T) in buying power.

And how you move their money into your Bitcoin wallet is by teaching them new skills, solving digital problems, and building bridges for them into the Native Digital world..

One of those skills is learning how to sell in the digital world.

We're not talking about going door to door selling phone books or bibles.

We're talking about helping businesses scale themselves on the Internet.

This could be everything from helping a local candle store setup an e-commerce site to aggregating lunch orders at your junior high or high school (in a Google doc) for a pizzeria to process bulk pizza deliveries for basketball or football games. Or what if you had other teenagers pay you $5 per week to go to the vintage candy store downtown, curate the best gummies and candies, and bring them a "grab bag" to munch on every Friday. Let's say half of that $5 is the cost of the candy and the rest is profit in your pocket. That is $250 per week x 36 weeks per school year = $9,000 each year or $36,000 before you turn 18.

Not bad.

The best part about offering to be a business's digital salesperson is that "digital sales" isn't really something you need to be qualified for. In fact, you can probably get yourself the gig just by taking it upon yourself to sell a local business's goods or services on your own, proving you can find customers, and then pitching them on how you'd like to be compensated going forward. For example: you can negotiate by saying, "Instead of paying me per hour, I want you to pay me per customer I bring into your store, or per product I sell." This minimizes the risk of the business (who wants to avoid adding another salary to their payroll) while simultaneously maximizing your earning potential. If you bring in very few customers, it's not a loss for the business. But if you bring in a lot of customers, that's good for the business and *very good* for you.

2

Radical Idea #2: Become a local business's best (digital) marketer via social media.

Since you are a Native Digital, you understand things about the Internet your parents and many other Native Analogs do not.

As a result, many Analog business owners will frequently look to hire teenagers and college students to manage their social media or digital marketing efforts. For one, they assume teenagers and college students will be cheaper than trying to hire a "digital marketing expert" in their 30s. And second, they assume just because you use TikTok and Instagram and Snapchat that you understand *how to market* on TikTok and Instagram and Snapchat.

Both of these assumptions are false.

A) Just because you are a teenager doesn't mean you should be paid minimum wage.

Take that thinking and walk the plank with it—right now.

Instead, we want you to internalize something very important: everyone in the world gets paid what they negotiate. Period. And contrary to popular belief, negotiating isn't about puffing your chest out and acting confident or pulling off some stupid *Wolf of Wall Street* "sell me this pen" sales trick. It's about understanding the value you provide, the urgency of the problem you're solving, and how valuable you solving that problem is to the person you're talking to.

- If the problem you're solving is low-impact and low-urgency, you are going to be paid very little.
- And if the problem you're solving is high-impact and high-urgency, you are going to get paid a lot.

People who solve big problems and deliver big value make big money.

This is how the world works.

So, with this in mind, how impactful would it be if you helped an Analog business that was selling nothing online suddenly start selling their goods and services digitally? Probably a lot. Especially if you could find a way to measure your impact and show the Analog business owner that your posts on TikTok or Instagram increased the business's revenues by 20%.

And then think about what happened at the start of the pandemic, when a lot of Analog businesses had to shut down. What was the sense of urgency for them to start selling their goods and services digitally? Very, very high. (And the truth is: their urgency is still, and will continue to be very, very high—because the world is becoming increasingly digitized.)

B) Just because you use social media, doesn't mean you have the skill of marketing on social media.

One of the big lies society teaches young people is that you get paid for your *time*.

That's not true.

As we said above, you get paid for the difficulty of problems you can solve, and the impact solving those problems has on someone else's business and life.

Most teenagers are great consumers of social media, but are not very proficient creators or marketers. And as soon as the business figures this out, your marketing gig is going to disappear.

Instead, we encourage you to stop treating social media as a TV in your pocket, and start seeing it as a digital video game that, when mastered, will allow you to print money from anywhere in the world.

For example, let's say you pitch the local candy store on being their digital marketer. You are already selling candy to lots of kids at your school (being a great salesperson), but you want to take things to the next level. You know what types of candy 100+ of your fellow students prefer. What else can you do with that information? Maybe you get curious and you realize that hard candies are popular for *kids with braces* since they can't chew gum or gummy candy. We'd encourage you to do some research, survey more students at your school, and turn that into a list of several thousand kids who are your friends or friends of friends, all of whom know that when they tell you they got braces, you'll have hard candy coupons coming their way (via the candy store).

Now imagine that you have this list of thousands of kids and you ask them to take before/after photos not just of their teeth, but of their candy preferences and how braces changed the types of candy they can and enjoy eating. This would make for pretty compelling social media content, don't you think? Not because it's "clever," but because it's designed to target a very specific type of Superconsumer: teens with braces.

By learning how to create content that attracts new and hyper-specific audiences to businesses, you can make serious bank for yourself (from your smartphone, in your sweatpants).

3

Radical Idea #3: Make a local business save money and become more efficient via digital software tools.

The third way to work with local Analog businesses is to *save them money.*

What makes most (Analog) jobs so unenjoyable are the inefficiencies you have to deal with on a day-to-day basis.

- Manually inputting data into an excel spreadsheet
- Having to send the same packages to the same list of mailing addresses over and over again
- Placing buy orders for the same products every couple days
- Flipping the same burger every day
- Answering the same dumb customer questions every day (When Pirate Christopher worked a retail job way back when, he and his co-workers kept a log of them.)
- Etc.

So instead of getting frustrated, get busy building a solution.

Every Analog business today needs help being digitized. There are currently 31.7 million small businesses in the United States. And the most popular industries are professional services, construction, retail, food service, real estate, manufacturing, and so on. For many of these businesses, orders can't even be placed online (must be over the phone or in person); confirmations are sent via paper mail; and there is effectively zero digital information dedicated to answer customer questions or complaints (and instead must all be handled manually, individually). If you are a teenager stepping into this sort of business, chances are, you feel like you've just been teleported thirty years into the past. It's grueling. It's annoying. And Nancy from accounting has a severe misunderstanding of how Facebook works (again, not her fault).

It can be easy to see these types of businesses as boring (and they are), but they power our economy.

We need dry cleaners.

And bicycle repair shops.

And bar & grill restaurants.

Which means, as a Native Digital, your biggest opportunity for financial upside is to help these Analog businesses evolve into the digital age.

Here's how big, and sometimes simple, the opportunity is: recently Pirate Christopher was watching football and drinking beer with a buddy when they decided it was time for pizza. In their town, the pizza choices are the major chains and two local pizza places, with just a few locations each. One has a modern website, with online ordering and a DoorDash integration for delivery. The other—*which was the one they really wanted to eat*—had a website from the 1990s, with just a menu and a phone number to call. So they called. The phone rang a lot. Someone finally answered. "You deliver right?" "No we don't." "But your website says you do?" "Sorry, we don't." So the pizza place with the great website and the DoorDash integration got the business. As insane as it sounds, in 2022 there are still janky websites and countless small restaurants losing buckets of bucks by not offering delivery or being digitally savvy. Often because the owner is too overworked to try and figure out how to build a modern website with a DoorDash integration.

When you think of ways to help an Analog business evolve into the digital age, remember to be a missionary and not a mercenary. Most high schoolers (and frankly all adults) go into a job search thinking, "How can I get paid for my time and labor?" That is how a mercenary thinks. **Instead, go in with a missionary mindset:** "How can I help you (small business) get paid through my unique insights, expertise, and experiences as a teenager? And how can I share in a small piece of that upside?"

If you walk in with that mindset, everyone will listen to your pitch. Remember: the people who make the most get paid because they create a lot of value *for others*, first.

So how do you help a company get paid?

Follow the money.

- Start with sales (current customers).
- Then marketing (potential customers).
- Then go to operations (helping the business save money).

The overarching goal is to figure out the fastest way to get the company paid. Because the faster the company gets paid, the faster you get paid. If you help them make or save money, they will value you (and therefore pay you) for it.

Odds are, there is an Analog business you frequent a lot already (making you one of their Superconsumers). It might be the bagel shop, sneaker shop, or coffee shop. Being a Superconsumer gives you instant credibility and a knowledge advantage—*"Oh, the double-shot mocha frappuccino is the bomb"*—which means you are already a qualified hire. Combine that with the fact you're a teenager who understands the Internet, smartphones, and probably every digital device on the planet, and all you have to do is find ways to help the business *get more business* or *save money within the business they currently have* and you'll have no problem getting paid.

Remember: most adults have a harder time learning new skills than you do. Which means your ability to learn new software tools is likely exponentially higher than the people you are working for—and thus more valuable.

For ideas here: look for all the things in the business that are manual and repetitive. Basically, all the boring stuff adults don't want to do and would hire teens to do. There is more than likely a software solution for that.

Think about their accounting and bookkeeping. Can you convert them to Quickbooks or Netsuite?

Do they pay people in cash, check, or direct deposit? You'd be surprised how hard it is for some Native Analog business owners to do things you find simple—like set up Venmo.

How do they manage their schedule of labor and who works what shifts? There are software solutions for that.

4

Radical Idea #4: Be your friendly neighborhood Geek Squad member for smart home devices.

As a Native Digital, you understand things your Native Analog parents, teachers, and family friends do not.

Like how to set up an Oculus.

Or how to create a Whoop profile and start tracking your daily performance health data.

Or how to connect your Peloton to a community leaderboard. Then connect the Peloton to Strava.

(And even if you've never done any of these things before, chances are you are capable of figuring it out in fifteen minutes after a few Google searches and 1-2 YouTube tutorials—whereas for your Native Analog parent, teacher, boss, or business owner this is the equivalent of being tasked with taking the ACT whilst inebriated.)

Most high-quality, best-selling Analog products these days have equally, if not more compelling Digital components.

For example: do you buy an electric mountain bike because the bike itself is "better quality," or because the bike gathers data while you ride and allows you to optimize your performance over time? The problem is, while most Native Analogs know how to order an electric mountain bike on the Internet, they have no idea how to get themselves set up in its new digital ecosystem—let alone make the most of the data they're gathering and learn how to interpret it in a way that enriches their experience.

There are services like Geek Squad (which mostly suck) that do help customers with this. They make roughly $15 to $20 per hour. But they can charge up to $50 for a 90-minute visit at home (which is about $34 per hour). Why not cut out the middleman, find someone you know (like your friend's parents) who would rather have you over than a stranger, mark it up to $75 per outcome ("I set up your Whoop") and call it a day?

Remember, you don't need a lot of customers. You just need a few awesome Superconsumers who love buying Analog products with Digital components but have no idea how to set them up. Imagine every time you went to hangout at your buddies' house, you went over a little early and their parents paid you $75 per product you helped them set up. Coaches and teachers would probably pay you to do the same. So would Grandma and Grandpa.

2 of these jobs per weekend equals $150 per week. $600 per month. Or just a little over $7,000 per year.

Which is all you need to hit $30,000 by the time you turn 18.

These are all tremendous opportunities for teenagers today.

5

Radical Idea #5: Round up your friends and form a team of Digital "Do Gooders" (and make even more money).

Building on the previous idea here...

The most effective way to create a highly profitable business, *fast*, is to niche down, then niche down again (then niche down again).

Be hyper-specific about what problem you're solving.

For example, instead of saying, "I'll help you set up your digital devices," pick one. Be the "I'll set your digital Peloton ecosystem & community up in 30 minutes" guy. Be the "I'll preload your Oculus with the best games for your family for Christmas" gal. The more specific you can be about what problem you are solving, the easier it will be for potential customers to think to themselves, "Hey, you know I was wondering what games we should put on the Oculus before wrapping it up as a gift—I can hire you to do that?"

Then, if you want to scale into more "niches," hire other

specialists to do great work on your behalf.

For example: turn your group of friends into a "scalable Geek Squad."

Imagine you start setting up people's devices and things are doing great. But taking a page out of Tom Sawyer here (*it's an old Analog book, don't worry about it*), let's say your friends see you rolling in the dough and want to join in. One might be the Peloton guy or gal. Another might be the Ring doorbell person. You find the customers, farm out the work to your friends, and take a cut across the board.

If you find 10 buddies to do more work for you, but you take 10% of their money (since you're the one bringing in the business), now you're making $14,000 per year.

Hey, that's more than enough to bank your $30K *and* buy a used car—or a heck of a lot of digital Fornite skins.

6

Radical Idea #6: Help optimize Zoom setups for your friends' parents who work from home.

We now live in a world where the vast majority of work conversations happen (and will increasingly happen) digitally.

But here's a problem most Native Analogs weren't prepared for:

"I know how to present myself professionally when I'm going to a real-life meeting. *But how do I present myself professionally when I'm going to a digital meeting?*"

If you are at all passionate about gaming, live streaming, or creating content on social media, then chances are you already know more about how to present yourself digitally than your parents, or their friends, or even the managers and Vice Presidents and executives at most billion-dollar companies. You probably have a better eye for lighting, or an understanding of which cameras to use for the best quality livestream, or how to position yourself at a desk so that the natural light from the window brings out the color in your eyes.

16

At the beginning of the pandemic in 2020, when the entire world had to start working remotely, Pirate Cole actually did this: he hired a gaming livestreamer 7 years younger than him to tell him which camera to buy and help him create his at-home streaming setup for work calls. He paid the "Zoom consultant" $150 per hour to basically give him an Amazon shopping list and then sit with him on FaceTime and tell him which cords to plug in, which settings to turn on and off, and a few lighting tricks to make his setup look pro grade. Pirate Cole then recommended him to five of his friends to do the same thing. (And Pirate Cole is a Native Digital! Now imagine how in-demand this service would be for Native Analogs who are fifty years old and have never hooked up an external camera to their laptop ever before in their life.)

There is a massive education gap between Native Analogs and Native Digitals as far as at-home Zoom setups go.

And this gap presents a wildly profitable opportunity for you.

The thing we want to emphasize here is that your biggest barrier to entry here is your own thinking. Most teenagers don't think of themselves as a "camera expert" or a "professional consultant." But the reality is, the simple fact that you understand how to do something most fifty year olds do not is what makes you an expert. And even if your only credibility is the fact that you've constructed your own streaming setup (so you can play World of Warcraft on Twitch.tv), guess what? That's more than all the Native Analogs who would love to hire you to help them do the same.

And even if you've never done this before, we bet you could

watch a few YouTube videos and figure it out. Challenge yourself to create your own Zoom/streaming setup for under $100 or $500 and prove you can do it. Then do it for your parents for free. Then ask them to introduce you to any of their friends or co-workers who want help doing the same. Ask your teachers if they need help too. And charge them $50 or $100 or $150 or more per hour.

7

Radical Idea #7: Leverage your sports/athletic experience and help local physical trainers/nutritionists build digital presences that would attract you.

There are an endless amount of smart, highly knowledgeable sports trainers, physical therapists, nutritionists, and coaches in the world who are experts in their respective fields but have absolutely no idea how to create a website, sell training routines online, or "do a TikTok."

And these Native Analogs are highly motivated to enter the digital world—they just don't know how.

Something you have to remember, as a teenager, is that you are someone's target audience.

- **Is there a physical therapy office in your town that works with all the local athletes and high school students?** If you are an athlete, you are their target audience.
- **Is there a nutritionist you know of that works with all the guys on your football team?** If you are on the football team, you are their target audience. (And even if you're not, and are on the hockey team, or baseball team, or are just health conscious, you are their target audience.)
- **Is there a soccer coach you know parents hire to work with their sons and daughters after school on drills and footwork?** If you play soccer, you are their target audience.

When you are someone's target audience, and you're conscious of it, you suddenly see all the things they could (and should) be doing that would get your attention (how they could be marketing to you). For example, if you were on the football team and trying to put on weight, wouldn't it be helpful for you if the town nutritionist made TikTok videos telling you what to eat? Or what not to eat? Or which protein powders and supplements you should take that are still healthy and good for you? Or, if you were experiencing an injury and in physical therapy, wouldn't it be helpful for you if the PT you were working with had an email newsletter that gave in-depth information on how to do your exercises for that week? Or included video lessons in the email newsletter that showed you how to do your exercises with perfect form?

You know what *you* would want.

So, go create it.

The easiest "sales pitch" in the world is for you to go to someone who wants to generate more business and say, "I am your target audience. If you did X, I would watch it every single day, and I'd send it to my friends encouraging them to watch it. And they would probably then want to come work with you too." This is every business's dream scenario. The problem is: many don't know how to ask for it—and even if they did, they wouldn't know how to go about finding someone to help them come up with the ideas, create the content, or help them bring their Analog knowledge into the digital world.

Be that person. (As a Thank You, they'll probably end up giving you your own services for free!)

8

Radical Idea #8: Thinking about medical school or law school? Ask to help your local doctors/lawyers digitize their mountain of paperwork and make money while you learn whether you want to pursue this career path.

While doctors and lawyers have high-paying jobs, they're also full of boring Analog tasks like paperwork, paperwork, and more paperwork.

But imagine how valuable it would be if you helped doctors and lawyers get set up with a distantl assistant in less than a week and automate away the parts of their jobs they hate most.

Or imagine templatizing the most repetitive parts of the job, finding a way to batch those tasks together, and then charging the doctor or lawyer $100 per hour to have you take them over and never have to worry about them again.

The secondary benefit of working with businesses and individuals *doing the thing you think you want to make your career* is you get to see first-hand what their day-to-day looks like. On the surface, being a doctor or a lawyer sounds like a great job—until you shadow a stressed-out doctor or lawyer with a full caseload around for a few weeks, or week, or even a day, and see all the other things they have to deal with. Now, you might have this experience and feel the greatest sense of fulfillment you've ever felt in your life, confirming your desire to take the Hippocratic Oath. Or, you might get two days into the work and say to your mom and dad, "Turns out, being a doctor sucks. I'm going to be a YouTuber instead."

Both are great outcomes: because now you know (based on personal experience) what you want out of life.

The opportunity here is to help busy professionals free up their time.

You can certainly help physicians, lawyers, and other white-collar professionals attract more clients and customers, market themselves online, or amplify their digital presence.

But the real problem every doctor, lawyer, banker, entrepreneur, and anyone who works for themselves has is called: *too many things to do, not enough hours in the day.*

Anywhere you can find and create efficiencies in this person's life is an opportunity to make some money.

9

Radical Idea #9: Learn Shopify and help a local physical store stand up an Ecommerce site.

Ecommerce is one of the most highly valued industries in the world—worth trillions of dollars.

So don't think of this as a "summer job." Think of it as an investment in a skill that will pay you dividends for the rest of your life.

Ecommerce could be anything from setting up a Shopify store, to selling digital products on Gumroad, to reselling objects on eBay and beyond. It's the art and science of selling goods online—physical or digital, products or services. Once you know how to "sell stuff" online, you possess a skill the vast majority of people on planet earth simply do not have. And if you know how to sell *your own stuff* online, then congratulations: you can skip college and proceed directly to the lambo store.

However, the easiest way to learn Ecommerce is on someone else's dime.

This is why we encourage you to start with a local business. Find someone who already has a solid product and just help them with the digital part—whether that means figuring out how to list the product for sale online (building a website or selling the product on a marketplace like Amazon, eBay, etc.), processing orders online, and receiving payments online. This removes the question of, "How do I create something people will want to buy?" and instead allows you to just work on building the skill of distributing that product in the digital world.

Once you figure out how to do that, the next logical step is to then sell and distribute your own products.

This could be anything from t-shirts to coffee mugs with funny sayings printed on the side to digital NFTs of animé cartoons you drew in your bedroom. In order to turn these products into cash, however, requires you to learn 4 different skill sets. Here's an example of a simple cash-generating flywheel you have all the resources to learn how to create for yourself:

- **Social Media:** This is your marketing flywheel. Whatever product you want to sell, create free versions of the product on social. If you're selling t-shirts, make videos of how you make the t-shirts, take pictures of your friends wearing the t-shirts, and educate viewers on why your t-shirts are *different.* If you're selling digital NFTs of animé cartoons, create timelapse videos showing how you draw the cartoons, post pictures of the beginning (sketch) and the end (painting) of the cartoons, and educate viewers on

25

why your cartoons are unique.

- **Website/Store:** There are dozens of website builders available today that are either freemium (free to start but cost money to unlock certain features) or cost as little as $10 or $20 per month to use. Squarespace. Wix. Shopify. OpenSea (for NFTs). Any of these will do. This is just somewhere for you to list your products for sale—a digital storefront.
- **Payment Processing:** This is how you collect your money in exchange for selling your products. Most, if not all of these website builders integrate with Stripe, Venmo, Apple Pay, and standard credit card processing platforms that easily connect to your bank account. If you don't have a bank account, you can also connect to PayPal.

These 3 things are all you need to start selling products online and making money.

And they can all be learned by reading a few articles on Google, watching a couple YouTube videos, and getting creative with the content you post on social media to attract your early customers.

10

Radical Idea #10: Help your local store accept digital payments via Venmo, Paypal, and Bitcoin.

Digital payments are a new language.

For most Native Analogs, the idea of money flying across the Internet still feels foreign, unsafe, and even a little scary.

But for you and your peers, *not* using digital currencies and digital cash platforms like Venmo is what seems weird.

Many Analog businesses today are missing out on potential revenue simply because they don't make it easy for younger generations to spend money easily with them. They don't accept Venmo or PayPal or Cash App. They don't accept Bitcoin or Ethereum. The question you need to ask is: why? Because "they're not allowed to?" Of course not. It's because they *don't know how*.

Which is an opportunity for you.

Pirate Christopher's father-in-law (an "old-old school" Native Analog) has a farm that, for the longest time, only took cash. (Like physical dollar bills—*can you imagine?*) After Pirate

Christopher's wife introduced him to Venmo, all of a sudden **50% of the farm's revenue was digital**. That's a pretty powerful outcome considering it probably took five or ten minutes to set up. So, look around: what other Analog businesses are missing out simply because they can't easily take credit cards, Apple Pay, Venmo, or Bitcoin?

You can take this one step further by educating these Native Analogs on how to not just accept digital currencies, but buy and hold the right ones.

For example: one of Pirate Cole's most successful entrepreneur friends (worth hundreds of millions of dollars) has what he likes to call a "cryptocurrency consultant." He was the one who first showed Pirate Cole's friend how to buy Bitcoin and Ethereum—and then once he got acquainted with those cryptocurrencies, he showed him how to start wrapping Bitcoin and Ethereum into other cryptocurrencies and get into "yield farming." Want to guess how old this "cryptocurrency consultant" is?

He's 17.

And everything he knows, he learned by watching YouTube tutorials and hanging out in Discord servers with other crypto enthusiasts.

You have to remember: the speed at which you can learn digital skills, tools, platforms, and languages is 100x faster than your Native Analog parents, teachers, coaches, and neighborhood authority figures. Which means you can basically pick any Native Digital topic in the world, invest 50 or 100 hours into learning it, and then turn right around and sell it back to the people around you.

Does your dad want to buy his first NFT?

Has your mom been thinking it's time to dabble into Bitcoin?

Go teach yourself how to do it, first. Then help them. Then their friends.

That's a new category of business—that you can start right now.

11

Radical Idea #11: Are you a senior and did you get into your dream school? Open source your course selection, extracurriculars, and test prep methods for future students to learn how you did it.

Another one of the fastest-growing industries in the world is digital education.

The e-learning market is currently valued at more than $250 billion (2021) and is expected to grow more than 20% each year for the next decade—which means by 2027, it will be valued at more than $1 trillion.

One of the most ridiculously profitable businesses in the world (that they don't teach you about in school) is creating online education materials & courses. Online education means no rent, no employees, and no fixed costs (like paper or printers or desks or chairs)—leaving you with an 80%+ margin business where your only costs are your own time, a few SaaS platforms to host the content, and the fees that get eaten up in payment processing. That's it. Even marketing is an optional spend (you can just market yourself for free on social media). In addition, and maybe an even bigger benefit of online education, is that your customer base isn't limited to your physical geography. Your students can be people anywhere in the world.

Now, you might be thinking, "Students? I'm a student! I'm not a teacher."

To which we'd say **ARRRRRRR!!!!!!!** *Everyone is an expert to someone.*

When you were in 3rd grade, who did you see as the experts? The 4th graders.

And when you were in 4th grade, who did you see as the experts? The 5th graders.

And when you were in 6th grade, who did you see as the experts? The 8th graders.

And when you were in 8th grade, who did you see as the experts? The freshman in high school.

Thinking about education as an adult/child relationship is outdated.

The way education works today is teacher/student, and the word "teacher" really just means "anyone with knowledge to share to their former self." If you're a freshman in college, you can be a teacher to a senior in high school. If you're a senior in high school, you can be a teacher to a junior or sophomore or freshman. If you're a freshman, you can be a teacher to an 8th grader (or a whole class of 8th graders). And so on, down the totem pole.

So, what have you learned in the past year, two years, four

years, that you didn't know way back when?

Sell that.

- **Did you just get into your dream school?** Create education materials teaching other kids (a year behind you) with the same "dream school" how you did it—and how they can too.
- **Did you make a huge mistake picking the wrong classes your freshman year?**Create an online course teaching other students how to avoid the same mistakes—and educate them on which classes they should take instead.
- **Did you ace a class most students say is "impossible?"** Create the *Ultimate Guide To Getting An 'A' In Algebra 2/Trigonometry* and sell it. It's not cheating. It's you, paying it forward, providing ambitious students with more education materials. How could a school get upset at that? (And if they do, *here's a little pirate advice*: just keep it on the down-low and sell it after school.)

There is no better digital business you could build today than an education business. Pirate Cole has an education business called Ship 30 for 30 that teaches people how to get started writing online. Whether 10 writers or 10,000 take the course, almost nothing changes. It's a digital, frictionless, automated, highly scalable business that can be run from a laptop.

Not a bad gig, huh?

12

Radical Idea #12: Create a guide of "everything you need to know" for incoming freshmen.

A business is just a mechanism for solving someone else's problem.

Well, as you probably know, schools are filled with problems. Which means, every single day, you are surrounded by potential business opportunities. (Other people's problems = your biggest opportunities.) Your peers have problems. Your teachers have problems. The school itself has problems. Employees of the school have problems. The parents of the students have problems. And all these problems can be yours to solve.

One of those problems is not knowing which classes to pick.

Another one of those problems is not knowing which clubs are worth the time and which ones aren't.

Another one of those problems is not knowing the right way to ask someone out to prom ("If only I could see some examples!!!").

Another one of those problems is not knowing how to manage your time as a student athlete or musician.

All of these problems are things your peers spend hours and hours worrying about—and because they worry about them, so do their parents.

Which is an opportunity for you.

Imagine how helpful it would be if a graduating senior created an Ultimate Guide To Surviving High School, specifically for incoming freshman in *your* town. After all, who better than you to create it? You survived high school—which makes you an expert. And you probably made a lot of mistakes, and learned a lot of hard lessons, that you probably could have avoided (if only someone had given you An Ultimate Guide To Surviving High School).

$10 Ultimate Guide x 1,000 incoming freshman = $10,000 every year, year after year.

Not a bad business.

But why stop there?

You can also create a $7 *Inspiration Guide: 30 Ways To Ask Your Date To Prom*, where all you do is curate the most creative ways people asked their dates to prom over the years at your high school, dig up pictures, and throw it all together into a Google Doc and export it as a PDF. (And for $27, parents can buy the print version—which you go and print off at your local Kinkos or FedEx.)

You can also create a high-touch consultancy service where you work with parents and students to help them pick the right classes their freshman year, together. You do a 30-minute "interests interview" with the teenager, get a sense for what he or she enjoys and wants to learn, and then you come back with a whole class itinerary you think would be a good fit for them. Package it together and call it $299 for a custom class schedule.

The ideas here are endless.

13

Radical Idea #13: Are there limited parking spots at school? Create a "local Uber" to match drivers with students who need rides.

Another problem that exists at school: parking.

First of all, half the students in high school aren't old enough to drive.

Second, of the students who are old enough to drive, some are still working on getting their driver's licenses.

Third, of the students who are old enough to drive and have their licenses, only some have access to cars.

And fourth, of the students who are old enough to drive, have their licenses, and have access to cars, there's still the question of available parking spaces.

So why not create a ride-sharing system for your school?

Find the students who have cars and parking spots—they are your "supply." Then go survey students who ride the bus, get dropped off by their parents in the morning, walk to school, or constantly complain about not being able to find a place to park—they are your "demand." And then create a public Google Doc where students can sign up for which days they want a ride and pay a fee (busy parents will gladly pay $20 per week if it means they don't have to drop their kids off every morning). Then go to the drivers and tell them how much they can "earn" by picking up a few extra students on their way to school, and take your percentage fee for coordinating the whole shabang.

And if it's successful... find another go-getter at a nearby school and franchise out your model.

Teach them how to do it and collect a royalty.

14

Radical Idea #14: Create content about the content you love so much.

It took *Squid Games* a month to reach 100 million viewers on Netflix.

It took MrBeast 4 days to reach 100 million viewers on YouTube.

In today's world, the content about the content can often be as (if not more) valuable than the original content itself. You don't just watch LeBron James play basketball—you also watch SportsCenter afterwards. You don't just watch The Bachelor on ABC—you also watch all the YouTube reaction videos and TikTok recaps and memes on Twitter. *Content about the content* can even be as extreme as watching YouTube videos of creators react to YouTube videos by other creators—all of which certain audiences find tremendously interesting, entertaining, and worthwhile.

Instead of just being a consumer of media, we encourage you to be a creator.

The creator economy is booming, and as a Native Digital, you are in the perfect position to capitalize.

However, this means changing your social media habits from straight consumption to treating it as a craft, a passion, a skill, and even a job. Instead of just watching your favorite YouTubers, how can you react to their content—and create content about the content? What's stopping you from creating your own channel where you recap what your favorite eSports players' best trickshots in Call of Duty? If you're obsessed with The Bachelor, why not create a channel where you make predictions about the show's contestants and allow viewers to create their own "Fantasy Draft" speculating on the show's outcomes with you? Or be like Celeste Barber and become one of the most successful digital comedians by making legendary parody videos. Or if you love watching viral videos, why not create an Instagram page that curates the best viral content on the Internet (like @TheFatJewish, who now has over 10 million followers on Instagram alone)?

By the way: creating content about the content you love so much is a terrific excuse to continue consuming your favorite type of content.

"Mom! I'm doing research for my next video!"

15

Radical Idea #15: Be the "I'll return your stuff on Amazon" guy or gal.

How annoying is it to return things online?

(Hint: it's very annoying.)

Always remember: things that other people find annoying are opportunities for you to make some extra cash (or, in some cases, a lot of extra cash).

According to Forrester Research, 25% of items bought online are returned. That's more than $200 billion worth of goods that people need help sending back to Santa's Workshop. More importantly, what this research doesn't account for are all the goods people want to return but don't have the time to, forget to, or simply decide the time it takes to return the item isn't worth the cost (not everyone wants to spend an hour out of their day returning a $50 item).

This is a business.

Start with your parents, neighbors, and friends.

But surely word will spread: "Hey, Sarah? I hear you return people's stuff on Amazon. I have a whole closet of stuff I've bought that never got around to returning—can you help?"

Then imagine what you can do around the holidays: run an end-of-December promotion where a family can batch all their returns together, put them in a box, and you come pick them up from their house—and process all their returns in just a few days. Done correctly, you could make the same (if not more) just in the month of December as you do the entire rest of the year!

16

Radical Idea #16: What data are you naturally throwing off in your personal life that can be leveraged and monetized?

The vast majority of teenagers in the world have no idea how valuable their spending habits are to big companies.

- Banks, credit card companies, and big retail chains desperately want to know what you (and all your friends) are spending your money on.
- Film studios want to know what movies and TV shows are most popular at your school.
- Book publishers want to know what you're reading.
- Streetwear brands want to know what songs are on your favorite Spotify playlist.
- Gaming companies want to know which Twitch.tv channels you consume the most.

And so on.

The reason is: companies pay big money to know what products your demographic loves. After all, it's the young people who set the trends, and act as a "canary in the coalmine" for where the world is likely going to change next. For example: the moment you see all the kids at your school trading in their iPhones for some other company's new smartphone device, you should probably tell your mom and dad it's time to sell Apple stock.

So, what data are you naturally accumulating that would be valuable to a big company?

Radical transparency here is a mammoth opportunity.

One of the creator business models we love (and have adopted ourselves) is creating a paid newsletter via Substack. Well, what's stopping you from creating your own paid newsletter where you publish radically transparent financial insights from you and your group of friends? Each week, you publish screenshots of your debit or credit card statements (just the purchases, not your personal banking info—obviously) and explain what you're spending your money on and why: "I bought these in-app purchases because..." is a goldmine of information to the right company (whose marketing department would *gladly* pay for a subscription to your newsletter).

Transparently share what apps you use, what TV shows you watch, what YouTube channels you think are rising or falling in popularity, and so on.

Your opinion matters.

17

Radical Idea #17: What do teens discover well in advance of adults? Curate that.

Don't want to be a creator?

Be a curator.

One of the best examples of how being a curator of information can lead you to a life of fame, fortune, and freedom is Tim Ferriss. In 2009, he wrote a book called *The 4-Hour Work Week*, which helped him launch his own podcast where he went on to interview leaders in every industry imaginable. Who is Tim Ferriss? It doesn't matter. He's not really the star of the show—and has since built an incredibly successful career curating other people's thoughts, insights, perspectives, and stories by category. For example, his book *Tools of Titans* is nothing but one big collection of habits, tactics, and routines of billionaires and world-class performers.

He's not the expert.

Instead, he's the expert of curating experts.

Monetize your unique ability to curate information before it becomes "mainstream."

Do you love discovering new music before anyone else? You can create a social media channel where you help other music fans find the next hit song early, too—and maybe even a service where someone pays you to help them assemble the perfect playlist for a specific mood (a playlist for running, a playlist for studying, a playlist for getting over a breakup, etc.).

Do you love watching viral videos on YouTube and TikTok? You can create a website, a newsletter, or a service that shares these viral videos with big social media channels or even news stations (they're always late to the viral video party) before they blow up. As an upsell, you can even chop these viral videos into snippets so other big pages have multiple pieces of content to share over the next week/month.

Do you love following streetwear drops? You can buy streetwear early and then go to your school and sell the rare pieces for 25%, 50%, 100%, even 200%+ more than what you paid for them. Flip collectable sneakers, sweatshirts, and stickers for a profit.

The point is: you are in a unique position to monetize your knowledge, passion, and access to whatever it is you love consuming. You know "that thing" better than anyone else. So, either help people get up to speed, or capitalize on the knowledge gap and buy early when it's low and sell later when it's high.

18

Radical Idea #18: Turn your costs into revenue generating machines.

The very last idea we want to leave you with is this:

Don't just buy things. Buy things that can pay you back (and then pay you a dividend long until the future).

Most people live their entire lives purely as a consumer. They want a guitar, they buy a guitar. They want a car, they drive their car. They want a camera, they use their camera, they forget about their camera, they throw away their camera. Objects are seen as things to buy, use, and then get rid of or replace.

But we'd like to introduce you to a different way of thinking.

When you're young, everything you buy matters. You have a limited amount of money, which means you can only buy so many things. So, how do you make the most of your capital? You buy things that will pay you back.

For example:

- **Don't just buy a guitar to play.** Ask yourself how you can turn this passion of yours into a revenue stream. After you take some lessons, can you turn around and help other people get started playing guitar? Can you create guitar-related content online and build an audience you can monetize? Can you take good care of your guitar, learn how to fix it, and then charge other people to fix their guitars?
- **Don't just buy a car.** Turn that car into a revenue-generating machine. Can you drive Uber? Can you rent seats to other kids at your school who need rides? Can you deliver Postmates? Can you rent it out on Turo?
- **Don't just buy a new computer to play video games.** Challenge yourself to turn your computer into a digital cash-printing machine. Can you teach yourself how to build websites, landing pages, or automated email sequences? Can you launch a Shopify store? Can you sell NFTs on OpenSea? How can you turn your new computer into a business?
- **Don't just buy a new watch to wear.** Do your research. Buy a watch that is going to appreciate in value and then flip it. Educate other teenagers in your town (or online) about watches. Turn your passion into profit.

This is how you exit the vicious cycle of just being a "consumer," and start living a life of financial freedom as a creator.

19

These are just 18 radical ideas to get you started.

But there are hundreds, if not thousands more out in the world.

We hope this mini-book has not only given you a place to start, but helped get your wheels spinning on how to discover these types of new business category opportunities for yourself.

Remember: all you need is $30,000 by the time you're 18 and, invested well, you have essentially guaranteed yourself a comfortable retirement.

And the skills you learn along the way will pay you dividends for the rest of your life.

Subscribe To Category Pirates

Did you enjoy this "mini-book" on category design?

We would love for you to hop aboard the pirate ship and join us.

You can subscribe to Category Pirates here: https://categorypi rates.substack.com

Each week, we publish a "mini-book" like this (5,000 to 10,000+ words) and send it straight to your inbox. And while we republish our "mini-books" on other platforms (like Amazon), the Category Pirates paid newsletter is our primary destination. There, our "mini-books" are more interactive, and we are better able to connect with readers like you directly.

In addition, you will receive access to our entire archive of "mini-books," full of frameworks, stories, and case studies on how to design & dominate new categories in the world.

We hope to see you aboard the pirate ship!

Made in United States
Orlando, FL
21 January 2022

13841053R00043